THIS BOOK BELONGS TO

Written by James Clements

PUFFIN BOOKS

UK | USA | Canada | Ireland | Australia
India | New Zealand | South Africa

Puffin Books is part of the Penguin Random House group of companies
whose addresses can be found at global.penguinrandomhouse.com.
www.penguin.co.uk   www.puffin.co.uk   www.ladybird.co.uk

Penguin
Random House
UK

Roald Dahl quotations from *Fantastic Mr Fox* (1970, 2022), *The Enormous Crocodile* (1978, 2022),
George's Marvellous Medicine (1981, 2022), *Danny the Champion of the World* (1975, 2023),
Charlie and the Chocolate Factory (1964, 2022), *Roald Dahl's Marvellous Joke Book* (2012), *The BFG* (1982, 2022),
James and the Giant Peach (1961, 2022), *The Giraffe and the Pelly and Me* (1985, 2022), *The Witches* (1983, 2022),
Matilda (1988, 2023), *The Twits* (1980, 2022), *Esio Trot* (1990, 2022), *Revolting Rhymes* (1982, 2023)
and *The Magic Finger* (1966, 2022). All titles are published by Puffin Books.
First published 2025
001

Printed in China

The authorized representative in the EEA is Penguin Random House Ireland,
Morrison Chambers, 32 Nassau Street, Dublin D02 YH68

A CIP catalogue record for this book is available from the British Library

ISBN: 978-0-241-61119-7

All correspondence to:
Puffin Books
Penguin Random House Children's
One Embassy Gardens, 8 Viaduct Gardens, London SW11 7BW

ROALD DAHL

Wonderful
Words
for Writing

WELCOME, WONDEROUS WRITERS!

Do you love words? Do you love writing?
You do? Then this is the perfect book for you!

In this book, you'll meet a *gigantuous* number of new words and learn how to weave them together to write *gloriumptious* stories of your own. Along the way, there are lots of fantabulous characters and examples from Roald Dahl's books to help you bring your own characters to life through language.

This book is chock-full of activities, hints and tips to help you become a word-wizard. You will soon be creating tales that will have your reader *churgling* with delight.

All you need to do is add some imagination of your own.

HOW TO USE THIS BOOK

You don't need to read the pages of this book in order - you can jump to the sections you find most interesting or the ones that will help you with the story you're writing at the moment. The activities on each page are there to help you to think about your own storytelling. If you are struck by a good idea for a story, you might want to pause the activity and get writing! As well as lots of new words, each section has writing examples to help inspire you.

In the final section (pages 84–95), you'll find pages of words and phrases to help you write your own stories and complete the activities in this book. You can dip into these pages whenever you need to.

Are you ready? Let's *gobblefunk* around with words!

CONTENTS

WONDERFUL WORDS

Words are the building blocks of writing. By choosing exactly the right words (or even inventing new ones), you can entertain, delight, scare or amuse your reader.

You can learn new words in all sorts of places, like talking to friends, on TV, in school and in magazines. Think of some places where you've learned new words. Write the places below.

Word Jar

The BFG kept the dreams he caught in a jar until he needed them. Add your favourite words to the Word Jar to keep them safe for when you need them!

Remember, you can always come back and add a new word to the jar when you come across it in this book or anywhere else.

SENSATIONAL SYNONYMS

Synonyms are words that mean the same thing – or almost the same thing –
as one another. For example, "big" and "huge" are synonyms.

Choosing the right synonym adds variety to your writing and can create a
fantabulous picture in your reader's imagination.

Look at how Roald Dahl describes the smell of the farmers in *Fantastic Mr Fox*:

Boggis gives off a <u>filthy stink</u> of rotten chicken skins.
Bunce <u>reeks</u> of goose livers, and as for Bean, the <u>smell</u> of
apple cider hangs around him like <u>poisonous fumes</u>.

Compare this to a version that repeats the same words each time:

Boggis gives off a <u>nasty smell</u> of rotten chicken skins.
Bunce <u>smells</u> of goose-livers, and as for Bean, the <u>smell</u> of
apple cider hangs around him like <u>nasty fumes</u>.

Which version do you think is better? Why?

_____

_____

How many synonyms
for "fantastic" can you
think of to describe
Mr Fox?

amazing

fantastic

Why do you think Roald Dahl chose to describe Mr Fox as *fantastic*?

Draw a picture of Fantastic Mr Fox, then write a description of him. Make the words in your description as varied as possible. Look back at your ideas on the opposite page for help.

WONDROUS WORD CLASSES

Nouns, adjectives and verbs are important word classes (types of words) that you can use to help make your writing extraordinary. Nouns are used to name people, places and things. Adjectives are words that describe the nouns. Verbs are action words, but they can also describe how the action happens.

Nouns

Write three nouns under each heading – A, B, C and D.

A – PEOPLE	B – ANIMALS	C – PLACES	D – OBJECTS

Now add your nouns in the gaps to complete these sentences. Check the letter under each line to see which category to choose your nouns from.

_____ went to _____ with a _____
      (A)   (C)   (B)

The _____ ate a bowl of _____ sitting in _____
    (A)   (D)   (C)

_____ was chased by _____ carrying a _____
      (A)   (B)   (D)

all the way to _____ .
        (C)

Underline your favourite sentence. Circle the silliest sentence. How could you make a story from one of these sentences?

_____

_____

_____

Adjectives

Underline the adjectives in the passage below from *The Enormous Crocodile*.

The Enormous Crocodile grinned, showing hundreds of sharp white teeth.

"For my lunch today," he said, "I would like a nice juicy little child."

Think of some other adjectives to describe the nouns in this passage, and write them below.

The _____ Crocodile grinned, showing hundreds of

_____ _____ teeth.

"For my lunch today," he said, "I would like a _____

_____ child."

Verbs

Complete the sentences below by circling one of the verbs.

The Enormous Crocodile **walked** / **strolled** / **sprinted** / **sauntered** through the jungle.

The Roly-Poly Bird **flew** / **soared** / **sailed** / **fell** through the air.

The children **ran** / **sprinted** / **jogged** / **stumbled** away from the crocodile.

Think about how you chose each verb. How do your choices change the meaning of the sentence?

_____

_____

_____

HOMONYMS

A homonym is a tricksy word that sounds the same as another word but has a different meaning. There are two types of homonym: homophones and homographs.

Homophones are words that **sound** the same even though they are spelled differently and mean different things. "Groan" and "grown" are homonyms.
(George let out a <u>groan</u> when he saw how tall Grandma had <u>grown</u>.)

Homographs **look** the same on the page, but they mean different things. "Left" is a homograph.
(Danny <u>left</u> the garage and turned <u>left</u> up the road.)

Circle the correct homophone in each sentence.

*A steamy **missed / mist** was rising up now from the great warm chocolate river.*

*The most tremendous noise of splintering **wood / would** and broken tiles came from directly above their heads . . .*

*"If you tried chewing one of these Gobstoppers here you'd **break / brake** your teeth off!"*

*"Here – take the money and run down the street to the nearest shop and **bye / buy** the first Wonka bar you see."*

Read the clues below. What word (homograph) matches both parts of the clue?

a type of jewellery	a noise a phone makes
to be unkind	to say or do something on purpose
a flying mammal	a piece of sports equipment

Puns are jokes that work because a word sounds the same but has two meanings.

> **Why does Willy Wonka smile when he's asleep?**
>
> He's having *sweet* dreams!

> **How does Willy Wonka keep his teeth clean?**
>
> With candy*floss*!

Make up some jokes using the homophones below.

ball (a round toy) / **bawl** (to cry)

_____

_____

road (a place for cars) / **rode** (past tense of "ride")

_____

_____

grate (to shred into small pieces) / **great** (really good)

_____

_____

PREFIXES AND SUFFIXES

Adding groups of letters to the start or end of a word can change its meaning. These are called prefixes and suffixes. Learning these is an easy way to expand your vocabulary!

Prefixes come at the start of a word. The prefix "un-" changes the meaning to the opposite, such as in **un**happy and **un**kind. Suffixes come at the end of a word. The suffix "-less" means "without", as in the Ladder**less** Window-Cleaning Company from *The Giraffe and the Pelly and Me*.

Think of a new prefix to change the description of these characters. You can make up a new word or use a real one! Use the prefixes in the box if you need some help.

The _____ friendly octopus

The _____ ordinary carrot

The _____ happy monkey

The _____ powerful robot

The _____ clever inventor

un-   non-

super-   extra-

not-so-

Draw your favourite character from the list in the box below.

Put words and suffixes together to invent new words. (For example, Giraffe has an "extra-extendable" neck!) Write your new words below.

Root word	Suffix	New word
giant	-able	
creature	-wards	
squish	-less	
friend	-phobia	
cheese	-ment	
joy	-ness	
custard	-proof	
cuddle	-ize	
rocket	-ful	

Which of your new words give you an idea for a story? Write down some ideas below.

New word	Story idea

GLORIOUS GOBBLEFUNK!

Sometimes it's tricky to find just the right word for what you want to say, but you can invent a *swashboggling* new word of your own!

The BFG uses many invented words. Can you guess what they might mean?

"They is just moocheling and footcheling around and waiting for the night."

Moocheling and footcheling might mean

"You would be swallowed up like a piece of frumpkin pie!"

Frumpkin might mean

"How wondercrump!" cried the BFG, still beaming. [. . .]
"How absolutely squiffling!"

Wondercrump and squiffling might mean

Invent some words to match these definitions. You can use the word bricks below to help.

_____ : lighter than air

_____ : bright and multicoloured

_____ : the noise of a welly boot getting stuck in the mud

-erous   -some

bubble   float   -tial

muck   airy   squelch

bubble   rainbow

cloud   kaleido-   shiny

vari-   ooze   bright

feather   -atious

feather   multi-   -ous

colour   sludge   -able

pop

Writing challenge
Make up a story using as many of your invented words as you can!

RIP-ROARING RHYMES

Whether you add a rhyming poem in the middle of your story or use rhyming words for characters' names or descriptions, rhymes can make your writing sing!

Read the Centipede's poem from *James and the Giant Peach*, then underline the pairs of rhyming words using a different colour for each rhyme.

We may see a Creature with forty-nine heads

Who lives in the desolate snow,

And whenever it catches a cold (which it dreads)

It has forty-nine noses to blow.

We may see the venomous Pink-Spotted Scrunch

Who can chew up someone with one bite.

It likes to eat five of them roasted for lunch

And eighteen for its supper at night.

List as many rhyming words as you can think of for each of the six words in the shapes.

toes

knows, blows,

there

hen

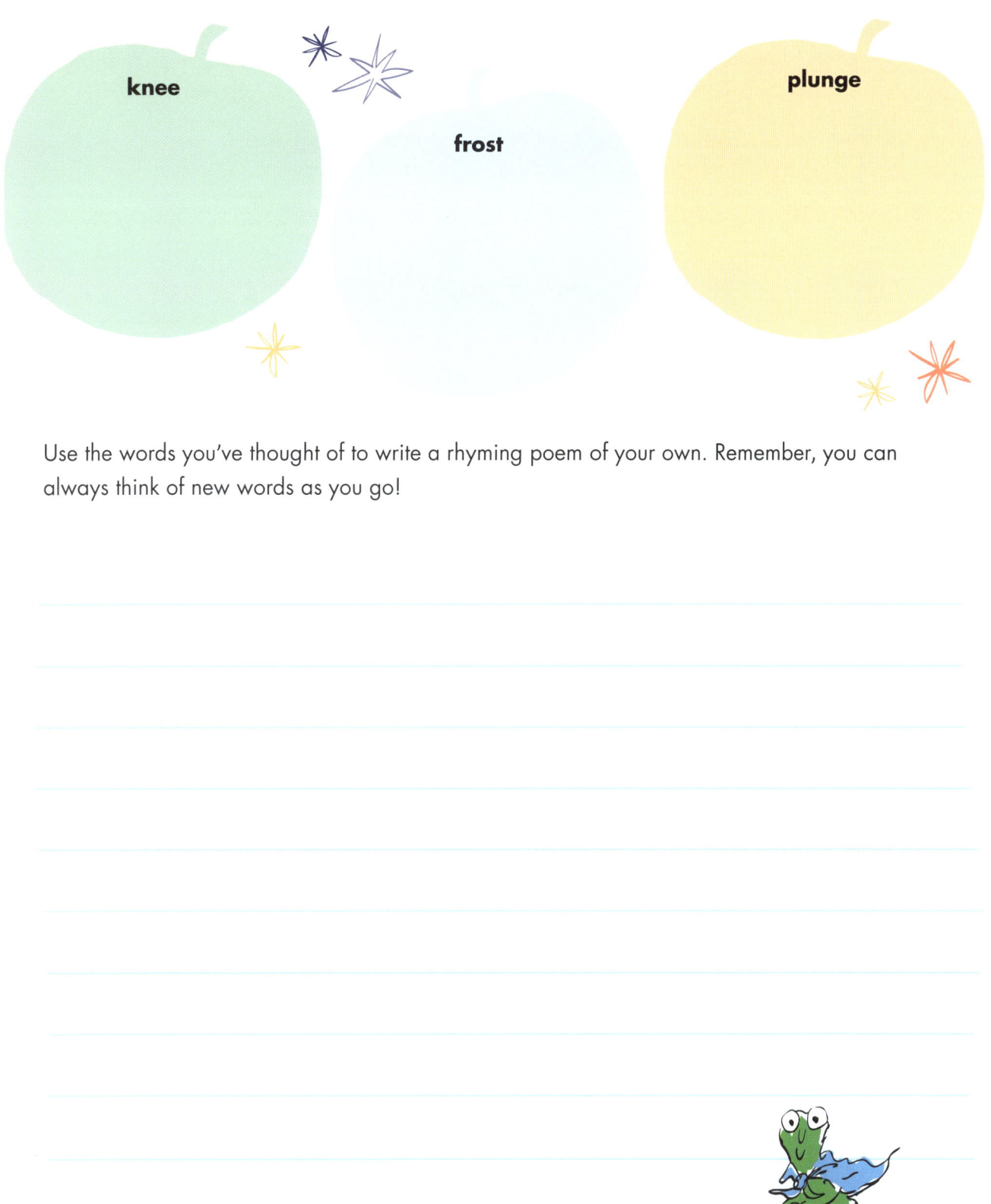

knee

frost

plunge

Use the words you've thought of to write a rhyming poem of your own. Remember, you can always think of new words as you go!

USING WORDS CREATIVELY

Now you've thought about the types of words you can use in your story, it's time to think about the *wondercrump* words themselves!

Write some words to describe your favourite things (they can be real or imaginary).

My favourite character from a book, TV programme, film or game is:

Words to describe them:

My favourite place is:

Words to describe it:

My favourite animal is:

Words to describe it:

My favourite food is:

Words to describe it:

The most magical thing I can imagine is:

Words to describe it:

CREATING CHARACTERS

To make your stories extra-brilliant, you'll need to include memorable characters – both brave and kindly heroes and *frightswiping* villains.

Underline your favourite adjectives in this description of Willy Wonka.

And what an extraordinary little man he was!

He had a black top hat on his head.

He wore a tail coat made of a beautiful plum-coloured velvet. [. . .]

Covering his chin, there was a small, neat, pointed black beard – a goatee. And his eyes – his eyes were most marvellously bright. They seemed to be sparkling and twinkling at you all the time. The whole face, in fact, was alight with fun and laughter.

And oh, how clever he looked! How quick and sharp and full of life!

Which words from the description above tell you that Charlie will like Willy Wonka?

Now imagine Charlie had met a **villainous** chocolate-factory owner instead! Think of some words that could describe this character.

Invent a new chocolate-factory owner, and draw a picture of them. Then use words from the box and words of your own to describe them.

Writing challenge

Write a new story starring your new character above, or use the words on these pages to invent a different character, and write a story about them instead!

SUPER SETTINGS

Inventing *spiffling* settings can help transport your reader to the world of your story and bring your writing to life.

Read the descriptions of settings from *The BFG*. Underline the words that tell you what the places look like, then draw a picture of each one.

Giant Country

Soon he was galloping over a desolate wasteland that was not quite of this earth. The ground was flat and pale yellow. Great lumps of blue rock were scattered around, and dead trees stood everywhere like skeletons.

The Queen's Palace

Not more than a hundred yards away, through the tall trees in the garden, across the mown lawns and the tidy flower beds, the massive shape of the Palace itself loomed through the darkness. It was made of whitish stone. The sheer size of it staggered the BFG.

Write a description of a different setting for a story. It could be a busy city, a jungle or even another planet, but choose your words carefully. You can use the words in the box if you need help. Then draw a picture of your setting.

towering	eerie	glistening	sandy	tranquil
majestic	soaring	winding	overgrown	modern
spectacular	hostile	narrow	barren	polluted
gloomy	menacing	powdery	lifeless	sprawling
shadowy	enchanting	pebbly	foaming	bustling

AMAZING ANIMALS

Furry or scaly, *gigantuous* or tiny, animals come in all sorts of different shapes and sizes. There are just as many *phizz-whizzing* words you can use to write about animals, too.

Here are some words you can use to describe animals. Look up the meaning of any words you haven't come across before. Add any more you can think of to the boxes.

Body parts		Movements		Sounds		Appearance	
tail	whiskers	hop	stampede	purr	chatter	aquatic	feathered
wings	shell	slither	bound	shriek	trumpet	hairy	elegant
beak	spines	glide	stalk	bellow	grunt	noisy	fierce
jaws	scales	slink	crawl	hiss	chirp	arboreal	slow
fur	tentacles	burrow	pounce	snort	bleat	smooth	long-necked
snout	antennae	scuttle	wiggle	growl	buzz	powerful	

Write some words to describe these animals from *The Giraffe and the Pelly and Me*. You can use the ideas above to help you.

The Giraffe, the Pelican and the Monkey are the perfect window-cleaning team.

The Giraffe replied, "I am the ladder, the Pelly is the bucket and the Monkey is the cleaner. Watch us go!"

With that, the famous window-cleaning gang sprang into action. The Monkey jumped down from the Giraffe's back and turned on the garden tap. The Pelican held his great beak under the tap until it was full of water. Then, with a wonderful springy leap the Monkey leaped up once again on to the Giraffe's back. From there he scrambled, as easily as if he were climbing a tree, up the long long neck of the Giraffe until he stood balancing on the very top of her head.

Invent a team of animals below. Draw the team in the box, then use words to describe how the animals would work together.

These animals are putting on a show at a theatre:

What they would each do:

FANTASTIC FOOD

Whether it's delicious or *rotsome*, real or imaginary, food can be a brilliant subject to write about in your stories because it really sparks the senses.

Willy Wonka invents the most wonderful confectionery in the world. Write descriptions of his creations, and then invent some creations of your own. Use the words at the bottom of the page to help you.

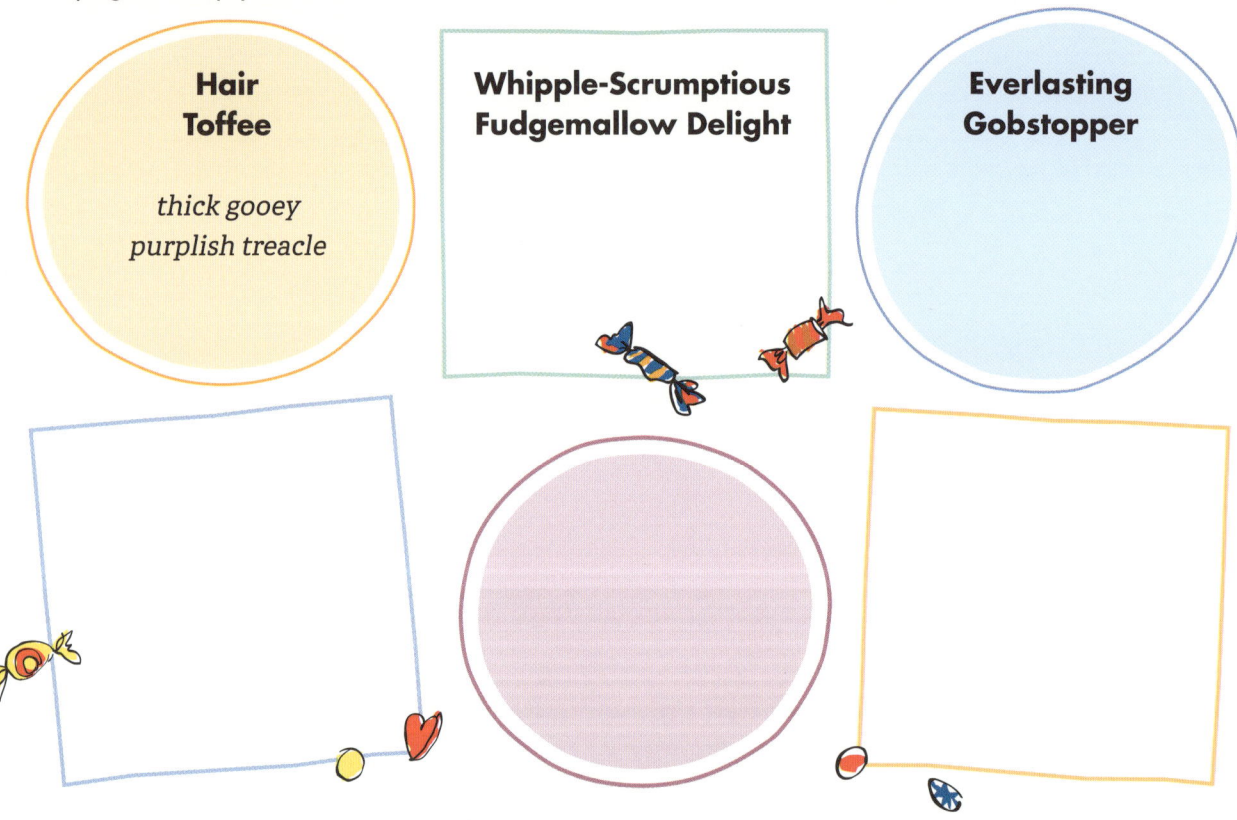

Hair Toffee

thick gooey purplish treacle

Whipple-Scrumptious Fudgemallow Delight

Everlasting Gobstopper

scrumptious-galumptious	rich	chocolate
delectable	delightful	marshmallow chews
crunchy	scrumdiddlyumptious	boiled gobstoppers
chewy	luscious	fudge
smooth	fragrant	caramel
creamy	flavoursome	nougat

Unfortunately, not all food is quite so delicious.

"It's disgusterous!" the BFG gurgled. "It's sickable! It's rotsome! It's maggotwise! Try it yourself, this foulsome snozzcumber!"

Write an advert to get people to buy *snozzcumbers*. Can you make them sound nice, or convince people that they're good for you?

Plan a menu of your own. It could be delicious or revolting. Remember to give your dishes brilliant names, and use as many words as you can to describe them.

STARTER

MAIN COURSE

DESSERT

MAGIC AND MISCHIEF

You can use magical and mischievous words to add a touch of enchantment to your writing and make your reader believe in your spellbinding words.

In *George's Marvellous Medicine*, George begins to sing a spell as he creates his magic medicine. Continue his spell using words from the box and words from your imagination.

So give me a bug and a jumping flea,

Give me two snails and lizards three,

And a slimy squiggler from the sea,

And the poisonous sting of a bumblebee,

Give me _____

_____

_____

_____

_____

_____

_____

powdered bone	**slimy stone**	**ghastly fruit**	**eyes of newt**
wombat's knee	**mouldy cheese**	**earwig tail**	**shell of snail**
poisonous sting	**bat's wing**	**beetles' brains**	**lions' manes**

Read the story text below from *The Witches*.

A witch never gets caught. Don't forget that she has magic in her fingers and devilry dancing in her blood. She can make stones jump about like frogs and she can make tongues of flame go flickering across the surface of the water. These magic powers are very frightening.

Describe some other things witches could do with their magic. Make your writing as bewitching as possible. You can use the words below to help you!

Witches can _____

_____

_____

_____

Words for doing magic:
cast spells, bewitch, conjure, invoke, sorcery, witchcraft, wizardry, charm, curse.

What magic might look like:
a puff of smoke, a flick of a wand, a bubbling potion, an incantation.

What spells might do:
make disappear, turn into a _____ , change the weather, summon, control, shapeshift, magic away.

Writing challenge

Write a magical story using one of the ideas on this page.

LOSING THE PLOT!

You've thought about the types of words and descriptions you might use in your stories, so now it's time to think about the words you need to put your fantastic story together.

Write down the names of some of your favourite stories. They might be told as books, TV programmes, films or computer games.

Fantastic Mr Fox

Why do you like them? Are they exciting? Funny? Clever? Scary? Think of the best words to recommend them to a friend.

Are there words or phrases in the stories which stick in your mind? Perhaps there are some brilliant descriptive words or a character who has a funny catchphrase? Write them below.

Isn't that fantastic!

Use your own words to describe your favourite moment in one of the stories.

STORY STRUCTURE

Most stories have a beginning, middle and end. The beginning introduces the characters and setting. In the middle, the characters often have a problem to solve. At the end, we find out how things have turned out for them. Choosing just the right words allows us to make our stories flow in the best way!

Read these phrases, and decide where they might be most useful in a story: write "beginning", "middle" or "end" next to each one. You might be able to use some in more than one place!

Leigh decided to do something about it. _____

The gate to the old house opened with a screech . . . _____

. . . and that was exactly what she did. _____

The world seemed different this morning. _____

And they all lived happily ever after. Or did they? _____

"Right, I've got a plan," said the captain, reaching for her map. _____

When Ash woke up that day . . . _____

But he was never seen again. _____

Later that day . . . _____

Use the story tunnel on the opposite page to plan your story with a beginning, middle and end. Use one or more of the phrases above for inspiration.

Think about:

- **who** your characters will be and **where** they live

- **what** problem they will face and **how** it is solved

- **how** things will turn out for them at the end.

Just like Mr Fox digging his tunnel in *Fantastic Mr Fox*, think of planning a story like travelling through a tunnel. As you enter the tunnel, consider how your story will start. Then think about what problems your characters will face in the middle. Finally, as you come out of the tunnel, decide how things will turn out in the end! Jot down any other words that will help you create your story.

STORY OPENINGS

Good stories need an exciting opening that captures the reader's attention. Use punchy and intriguing words to turn your introduction into a real *razztwizzler*!

Stories might begin with action, or they might hook the reader's attention by getting them thinking about what could happen next. Read the story text below from *George's Marvellous Medicine*.

"I'm going shopping in the village," George's mother said to George on Saturday morning. "So be a good boy and don't get up to mischief."

This was a silly thing to say to a small child at any time. It immediately made him wonder what sort of mischief he might get up to.

Which words suggest that George might do something he isn't supposed to do?

_____

_____

Underline the words below which also mean **mischief**.

high jinks   **tomfoolery**   **sensibleness**

seriousness   **mischievousness**   **shenanigans**

Could you use one of these words to help you think of a story of your own where the main character does something they're not supposed to? Plan your story below.

_____

_____

_____

At the beginning of a story, intriguing words can tell the reader lots about the main characters:

"And don't forget to give Grandma her medicine at eleven o'clock," the mother said.

Then out she went, closing the back door behind her.

Grandma, who was dozing in her chair by the window, opened one wicked little eye

and said, "Now you heard what your mother said, George. Don't forget my medicine."

Underline the words that tell you Grandma might not be a very nice character. Now look at the sentences below. What do the words tell you about each of the characters?

Sam sniffed and wiped his eyes.

The kitten barged straight through.

Dad squeezed Ali's arm gently.

Writing challenge

Use one of the story openings or characters from these pages to write a story of your own.

MARVELLOUS MIDDLES

The middle of a story is where the plot unfolds and new or exciting things happen to the hero. There is often a *biffsquiggling* problem to solve or an obstacle to overcome.

Think of as many action words as you can that indicate a tricky problem will occur in the middle of the story. Use the words in the box below if you need help.

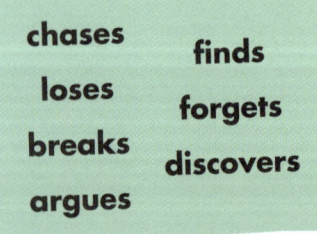

chases
finds
loses
forgets
breaks
discovers
argues

Choose the word you find most interesting, and use it to create a middle-of-the-story problem.

_____

_____

_____

_____

The middle of a story is often exciting! Read the scene below from *The Witches*, and think about how Roald Dahl makes it exciting. Find examples and write them in the boxes below.

Very carefully a victim is chosen. Then the witch stalks the wretched child like a hunter stalking a little bird in the forest. She treads softly. She moves quietly. She gets closer and closer. Then at last, when everything is ready . . . phwisst! . . . and she swoops! Sparks fly. Flames leap. Oil boils. Rats howl. Skin shrivels. And the child disappears.

Verbs showing the action	stalks,
Adverbs showing how action happens	
Repetition of words or phrases	
Short, exciting sentences	

Use the same techniques to write your own exciting scene. Choose one of these options, and write the scene below. Your main character could be:

being chased   **hiding from the villain**   **walking into a dangerous place**

_____

_____

_____

_____

_____

41

EXCITING ENDINGS

All stories need a good ending! It's important to plan out a resolution, where your reader finds out how things turned out for the characters in the end.

In lots of stories, the characters get the ending they deserve: the heroes get a happy ending, and it all ends badly for the villains. In *James and the Giant Peach*, James and the creatures he meets in the peach all make their own extraordinary ending together.

Complete these story endings with words that show the heroes got the ending they deserved. You can think of your own word or choose one from the box below.

The Centipede, who had so many _____, was put in charge of a company that sold

_____.

The Glow-worm, who could _____ became the light inside the _____
on the Statue of Liberty.

The Old-Green-Grasshopper, who _____ with his legs, became a member of an

_____.

James Henry Trotter, who had been very _____ as a child, had lots and lots of

_____.

lonely	**legs**
played music	**friends**
light up	**torch**
boots and shoes	**orchestra**

The Giraffe and the Pelly and Me ends with a song sung by the Monkey.

> We have tears in our eyes,
>
> As we wave our goodbyes,
>
> We so loved being with you, we three,
>
> So do please now and then,
>
> Come and see us again,
>
> The Giraffe and the Pelly and Me.
>
> All you do is to look,
>
> At a page in this book,
>
> Because that's where we always will be.
>
> No book ever ends
>
> When it's full of your friends,
>
> The Giraffe and the Pelly and Me.

Write the words and phrases that make you think this is a happy ending to the story.

Write the words and phrases that make you think this is a sad ending to the story.

Overall, do you think it is happy or sad? Explain why.

THE WRITER'S CRAFT

Exciting individual words are vital for your writing – but the real skill lies in weaving those words together to create amazing sentences. You can learn lots of special techniques from your favourite authors.

Choose a book you love, then look through it to find an example of some brilliant dialogue (where the characters are speaking to each other).

Choose one character, and write down some of the words they say.

_____

_____

_____

_____

_____

What do the character's words tell us about them and how they feel?

_____

_____

_____

_____

_____

Use what you have written on the opposite page to draw a picture of the character speaking.

"A fine writer will always make you feel that," Mrs Phelps said. *"And don't worry about the bits you can't understand. Sit back and allow the words to wash around you, like music."*

SHOW, DON'T TELL

Great storytellers don't need to tell their reader how a character is feeling – they use words that show feelings through the character's speech and actions.

In *Danny the Champion of the World*, Danny and his father sneak into the wood to poach some pheasants.

My father was [. . .] picking his feet up high and putting them down gently on the brown leaves. He kept his head moving all the time, the eyes sweeping slowly from side to side, searching for danger.

You can tell how Danny's father feels from the description of his walk. Underline all the words in the box below that show how he feels.

nervous	**happy**	**worried**	**strong**
angry	**tense**	**confident**	**cautious**

What words could you use to describe these characters' movements and also show how they're feeling?

A happy toddler running to his grandparents.

_____

An angry bear who's just been woken up.

_____

An athlete walking to collect her gold medal.

_____

In the story, Danny meets Mr Victor Hazell who owns the woods where the pheasants live.

> Mr Hazell had pulled up alongside the pumps in his glistening gleaming Rolls-Royce and had said to me, "Fill her up and look sharp about it." I was eight years old at the time. He didn't get out of the car, he just handed me the key to the cap of the petrol tank and as he did so, he barked out, "And keep your filthy little hands to yourself, d'you understand?"
>
> I didn't understand at all, so I said, "What do you mean, sir?"
>
> There was a leather riding crop on the seat beside him. He picked it up and pointed it at me like a pistol. "If you make any dirty fingermarks on my paintwork," he said, "I'll step right out of this car and give you a good hiding."

Choose three words or phrases from the story text above that show you what type of a person Victor Hazell is. Write them below.

What words would you use to describe Victor Hazell?

WRITING DIALOGUE

Writing excellent dialogue – when the characters in stories speak to each other – is an important skill to develop as a writer. Good dialogue should give the reader information about a character.

Sometimes the words themselves are enough to tell you how a character is speaking. Read the dialogue in the boxes below out loud. Underline the words that gave you clues about how to read it.

> "Ssshh!" said Grandpa Joe. "Listen!
>
> Here comes another song!"

Write some dialogue for the characters below.

Willy Wonka

Aunt Sponge and Aunt Spiker

Miss Trunchbull

Sometimes using a verb other than "said" can help:

"Wait!" shrieked one of the witches in the back row.

And sometimes an adverb tells us how a character says something:

"You mustn't be frightened," the Ladybird said kindly.

Read the speech below, and choose some **verbs** and **adverbs** to fill in the gaps.
Can you change the tone by changing how the character speaks?

"I think it's supposed to look like that," Sam _____ .

"I think it's supposed to look like that," Sam _____ .

"Oh, you found it did you?" Charlotte said _____ .

"Oh, you found it did you?" Charlotte said _____ .

"I want to go home," Violet _____ .

"I want to go home," Violet _____ .

boasted	bellowed	beamed	angrily	warmly
screeched	smiled	gasped	loudly	roared

DAZZLING DESCRIPTIONS

There are so many words to choose from. Picking vivid adjectives and adverbs to describe your characters and settings can make your writing sparkle.

In Roald Dahl's description of Mr Twit, carefully chosen words like *foul* and *horrid*, as well as descriptions of his actions, show just how unpleasant Mr Twit is.

> *By sticking out his tongue and curling it sideways to explore the hairy jungle around his mouth,*
>
> *he was always able to find a tasty morsel here and there to nibble on.*
>
> *What I am trying to tell you is that Mr Twit was a foul and smelly old man.*
>
> *He was also an extremely horrid old man, as you will find out in a moment.*

Underline all the words above that describe how horrible Mr Twit is.

Now label the picture below with some words and phrases that describe the other parts of Mr Twit. Try to choose interesting words.

nose

mouth

eyes

face

clothes

feet

In the space below, write lots of words and phrases to describe the Twits' house and garden.

Now use your ideas to write a dazzling description of their home.

USING YOUR SENSES

A great way to transport your reader to the world of your story is to call on the senses – sight, sound, touch, smell and taste. The more expressive the words you use when writing about the senses, the easier it is to imagine it's real!

Look at how words relating to sight and smell describe George's marvellous medicine bubbling on the stove.

Soon the marvellous mixture began to froth and foam. A rich blue smoke, the colour of peacocks, rose from the surface of the liquid, and a fiery fearsome smell filled the kitchen. It made George choke and splutter. It was a smell unlike any he had smelled before. It was a brutal and bewitching smell, spicy and staggering, fierce and frenzied, full of wizardry and magic.

Which sense would be sparked by each of the words below? Write them out in the correct columns. Watch out – some of them can go with more than one sense!

froth	**whiff**	**sparks**	**hiss**	**bright**	**crunch**
foam	**prickle**	**swirl**	**squish**	**creamy**	**bubble**
burn	**smoke**	**fumes**	**steam**	**bitter**	**sweet**

SIGHT	SOUND	TOUCH	SMELL	TASTE

Imagine inventing a marvellous medicine of your own. Can you think of some words and phrases to describe it? Remember to use a mixture of **nouns**, **verbs** and **adjectives**.

I would see . . .

I would hear . . .

I would smell . . .

I would feel . . .

I would taste . . .

Now use your favourite words from above to write a detailed description of your potion. Write about all five senses and make your description as vivid as possible.

METAPHORS AND SIMILES

A metaphor is a way to describe something by comparing it to something else.
A simile also compares two things but uses the word "as" or "like". Making your
metaphors and similes as imaginative as possible will help your writing stand out.

Read the story text below from *Esio Trot*.

*Mr Hoppy turned and ran from the balcony into the living room, jumping on tip-toe
like a ballet dancer between the sea of tortoises that covered the floor.*

Both **similes** and **metaphors** help the reader to imagine the scene.

Think of some more metaphors to describe Mr Hoppy's floor covered with tortoises.
Write them below.

a sea of tortoises

a carpet of tortoises

In the story, Mr Hoppy buys lots of tortoises of different sizes. Think of some similes to describe the biggest and smallest tortoises.

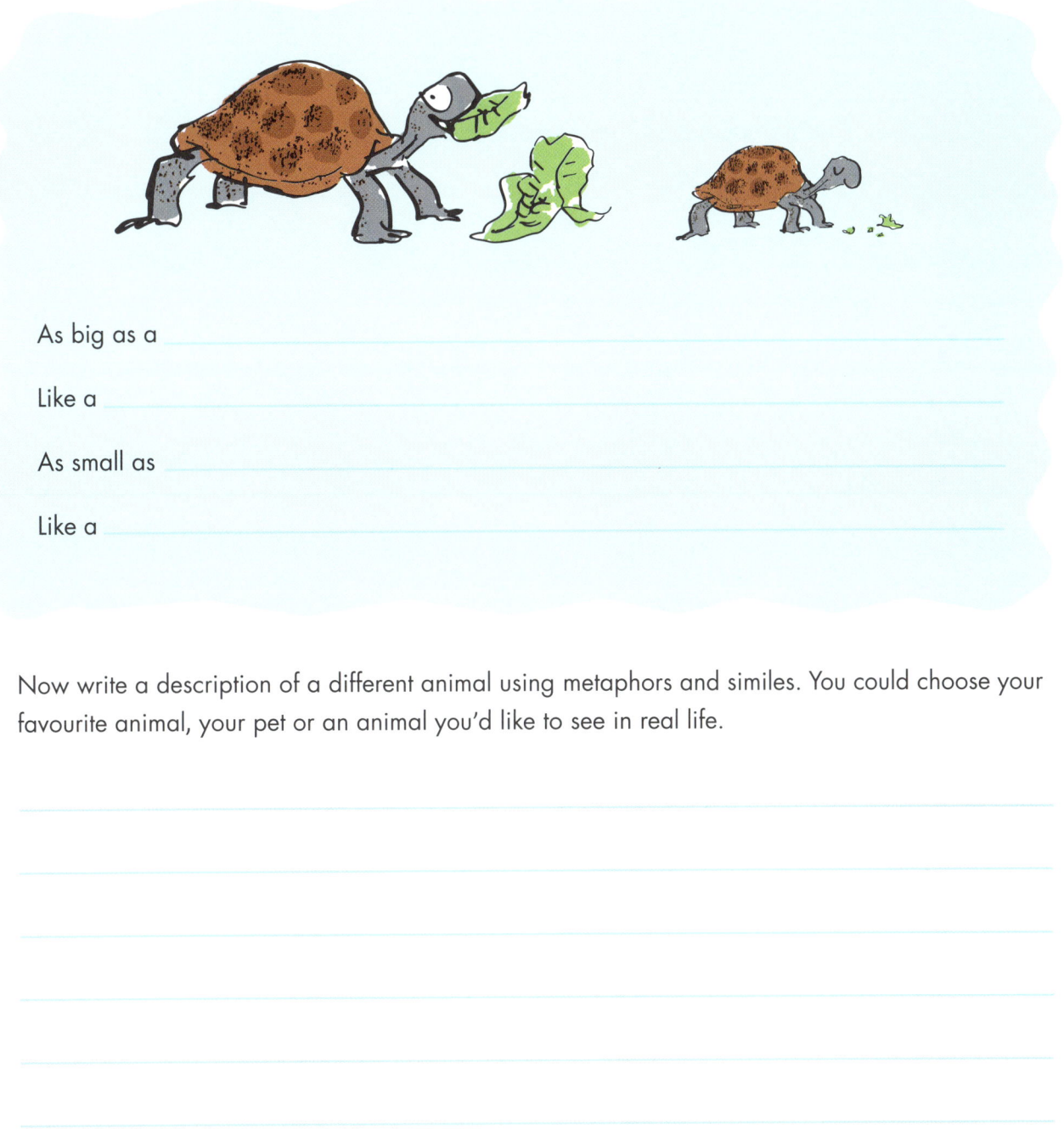

As big as a _____

Like a _____

As small as _____

Like a _____

Now write a description of a different animal using metaphors and similes. You could choose your favourite animal, your pet or an animal you'd like to see in real life.

_____

_____

_____

_____

_____

_____

ALLITERATION AND ONOMATOPOEIA

The meaning of the words we write is very important but so is the sound of the words! The right combination of sounds using alliteration and onomatopoeia can create music on the page.

Alliteration is where the same sound is repeated at the start of multiple words that are close together.

The <u>rotten</u> old <u>rotrasper</u>!

The <u>filthy</u> old <u>fizzwiggler</u>!

Circle the BFG's phrases that use alliteration.

"Every human bean is diddly and different"

"Your head is full of squashed flies."

"all over the wonky world"

"I is a very mixed-up Giant."

"Like a whiffswiddle!"

"This is a serious and snitching subject"

Can you think of any characters with alliterative names? Can you make up some of your own?

Use the words below, and some of your own, to write some sentences using alliteration.

grizzly	**wheelbarrow**	**buckswashling**
grobsludging	**whispered**	**bugs**
growling	**whirligig**	**bumped**
grinned	**wild**	**buddy**
grandpa	**wombat**	**butterfly**

Onomatopoeic words sound like the thing they describe, words for sounds and actions like "zoom" and "crunch", or "quack" and "moo". Underline the examples of onomatopoeia below.

"A dream," the BFG said, "as it goes whiffling through the night air,

is making a tiny little buzzing-humming noise. But this little buzzy-hum

is so silvery soft, it is impossible for a human bean to be hearing it."

Tiny little noises sound very loud to the BFG. Using onomatopoeia, describe what the BFG might hear on a quiet night.

I is hearing _____

I is hearing _____

I is hearing _____

GRAMMAR AND PUNCTUATION

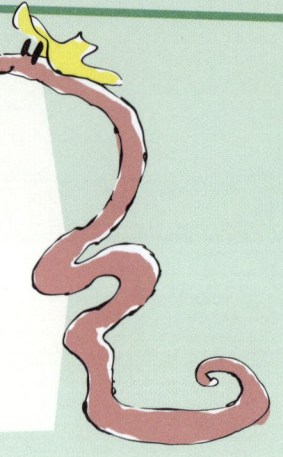

All these *phizz-whizzing* new words aren't much use without grammar and punctuation. It's the glue that sticks the words together, and sometimes it changes the meaning entirely.

How many different punctuation marks do you know already? Write some in the space below.

Which is your favourite one to use?

Write some sentences below using any of the punctuation marks that you already know.

Grammar and punctuation can be a *plexicated* business, so first think about what you know already using the opposite page.

Write down what you know about grammar and punctuation below. Don't worry if you're not sure about any sections – the next few pages will help you to fill in any gaps!

Statements, questions, commands and exclamations are all types of . . . _____

The present tense is when . . . _____

The past tense is when . . . _____

The first person is when . . . _____

We use full stops for . . . _____

We use exclamation marks for . . . _____

We use question marks for . . . _____

We use colons for . . . _____

We use semicolons for . . . _____

We use speech marks for . . . _____

We use apostrophes for . . . _____

PUNCTUATING SENTENCES

Now you know the different types of sentences, let's practise using some punctuation to add some impact to your words and make them clear to your reader.

Match the type of sentence to the correct punctuation marks.

Questions	Usually an exclamation mark
Statements	Always a full stop
Commands	Either a full stop or an exclamation mark
Exclamations	Always a question mark

Sentences start with a capital letter and end with a full stop, question mark or exclamation mark (boundary punctuation). Add the correct boundary punctuation to the scene from *The Twits* below, where Mr Twit has secretly made Mrs Twit's walking stick longer.

? ? ? . . . !

"What can have happened___" Mrs Twit said, staring at her old walking stick___ "It must suddenly have grown longer___"

"Don't be silly___" Mr Twit said. "How can a walking stick possibly grow longer___ It's made of dead wood, isn't it___ Dead wood can't grow___"

We can sometimes use different sentence types to create interest. We could ask a question to engage our reader.

Can you believe that Mr Twit stretched Mrs Twit with balloons?

Write two more questions about the Twits using these question words.

Did you _____

_____

Are you _____

_____

Adding an exclamation can also add variety.

"By golly it is a Giant Skillywiggler!" Mr Twit said.

Write two more exclamations that could be used in another story about the Twits. You can use some of the words below to help you.

_____

_____

_____

_____

| bellow | roar | raged |
| furious | beastly | nonsense | purple |

SUPERB SENTENCES

We can organize words into four main sentence types: statements, questions, commands and exclamations. Using a range of sentence types can help to add variety to your writing and make sure your reader understands the meaning of the words you've used.

Read the definitions of each sentence type, and write an example for each one. Remember to choose your words carefully to make your sentences as exciting and interesting as you can.

Questions   These sentences ask something. They always end in a question mark.

Statements   These sentences are used to share information or opinions. They usually end in a full stop.

Commands   These sentences tell someone to do something. They can end in a full stop or an exclamation mark.

Exclamations   These sentences show strong feelings. They usually end in an exclamation mark.

Draw lines to match each quote from *The Twits* to its sentence type:
statement, question, command or exclamation.

*With her feet tied to the
ground and her arms pulled
upwards by the balloons,
she was unable to move.*

*"If those strings around
my ankles break, it'll be
goodbye for me!"*

*"Are you sure my feet
are tied properly to
the ground?"*

*"Can you feel them
stretching you?"*

Statement **Question**

Command **Exclamation**

*"There's enough
pull here to take
me to the moon!"*

*"Put some more string around
my ankles quickly!"*

*He put on another
ten balloons.*

*With one quick slash,
he cut through
the strings.*

*She went up like
a rocket.*

*"At last the old crow is lost
and gone forever."*

"What a ghastly thought!"

SENTENCES FOR EFFECT

Organizing words into different types of sentences can create different effects.
Choosing just the right words to make your characters exclaim, command or
ask a question can all help you to make your writing interesting.

Write an exclamation, a command and a question for Mr and Mrs Twit, using the very best words
you can think of and matching punctuation. You can look for inspiration in the box below.

genius	horrible	brilliant	beastly	rotten
eye on you	filthy	terrible trick	arghhh!	swizzle

Weaving words into commands is useful when you need to give your reader instructions.

Plan a trick for Mrs Twit to play on her husband. Use commands to write some instructions for how to play the trick. Remember to break your instructions into simple steps, and use lots of verbs and adverbs so your reader can follow easily.

place	mix	roll	close	remember	make
fill	switch	tie	dig	fix	bend

USING SENTENCES

Now it's time for you to put your sentence knowledge to the test! Can you remember which words and punctuation to use for each sentence type?

Help! The text below has been written as one long sentence. Write it out again, breaking it into shorter sentences, and adding the correct punctuation.

Mr Twit caught a big frog by the pond and carried it home in a box and he put it in Mrs Twit's bed and when Mrs Twit got in she felt something cold and slimy crawling on her feet and she screamed and Mr Twit said it was a Giant Skillywiggler.

_____

_____

_____

_____

Punctuation and grammar are important, but the words you choose are even more important! Write some other ways of saying these phrases to make each one even more interesting and lively.

a big frog   a _____ frog   a _____ frog

he put it in Mrs Twit's bed   he _____ Mrs Twit's bed

he _____ Mrs Twit's bed

she screamed   she _____   she _____

Now circle the one you'd use from each row if you were writing a story.

Write what Mr and Mrs Twit might say to each other after Mr Twit's Giant Skillywiggler trick. You can use words you've learned from this book and words of your own. Try to use a range of statements, questions, commands and exclamations.

MRS TWIT:

_____

_____

_____

MR TWIT:

_____

_____

_____

MRS TWIT:

_____

_____

_____

MR TWIT:

_____

_____

_____

TENSE AND VOICE

The tense and the voice you choose can make a big difference to the feel of your story. Usually, the verbs tell the reader which tense we are writing in. Learning to change the form of verbs can make you a better storyteller.

The tense tells the reader when the action is happening. Changing the verbs changes the tense, like this:

Jack walk**ed** towards the beanstalk – past tense (it happened in the past)

Jack walk**s** towards the beanstalk – present (it's happening now)

Jack will walk towards the beanstalk – future (it will happen in the future)

Read the extracts below from *Revolting Rhymes*, and colour the sentences in different colours to show whether they are written in the past, present or future tense.

> When Jack produced one lousy bean,
>
> His startled mother, turning green,
>
> Leaped high up in the air and cried,
>
> "I'm absolutely stupefied!"

> The mother actually perceives
>
> A mass of lovely golden leaves!
>
> She yells out loud, "My sainted souls!
>
> "I'll sell the Mini, buy a Rolls!"

Change these examples of glorious *gobblefunk* words into the past and present tense.

ROOT	PRESENT TENSE	PAST TENSE
bopmugger	bopmuggers	bopmuggered
crodsquinkle	_____	_____
frothbungle	_____	_____
scuddle	_____	_____

Write a scene from a well-known story using a tense of your choice. Use your own words or borrow some from the box below (but watch out, you might need to change them to match your tense!).

fearsome	live	spring	roar	safety
sneak	forest	grin	hurtle	spell

COLONS AND SEMICOLONS

Colons and semicolons can be useful punctuation marks when you're weaving words and sentences to use in your stories. They can be used to join two parts of a sentence together and add variety to your writing.

Colons are used when the second part of a sentence explains, or elaborates on, the first part.

And that's when it happened: George's Grandma began to grow taller.

Add a colon to the right place in the sentences below.

Never forget I have wizardry in the tips of my fingers.

The medicine began to change bubbles and smoke rose from the pan.

But it was too late the ancient beanpole had swallowed everything in the cup in one gulp.

Now write a sentence of your own using a colon.

_____

_____

Colons can also be used to introduce a list. Add some more ingredients to the list.

He chose the following and emptied them one by one into the saucepan:

- *a tin of curry powder*
- *a tin of mustard powder*
- *a bottle of extra-hot chilli sauce*

_____

_____

You can use semicolons where you would use a word like "and", "but" or "so".

The hen seemed better; it stood up and flapped its wings.

Draw a line to join a part of a sentence from the first column, and another part from the second column, so they make sense.

George didn't say a word;	the big pan was still on the stove.
But Grandma didn't stop there;	soon it was four times its normal size.
Bigger and bigger, taller and taller it grew;	he felt something tremendous had taken place that morning.
George went into the kitchen;	she carried on right through the ceiling.

Now write your own sentence using a semicolon. Then draw a picture of what is happening below.

SPLENDID SPEECH MARKS

Speech marks, also called inverted commas, are used to show which words a character is speaking. This is so readers can tell the difference between a character's words and the words that are telling the story. It also means the reader can imagine the character's voice as they read the words!

"Do you know what I would like for my lunch today?" the Enormous Crocodile asked.

"No," the Notsobig One said. "What?"

The Enormous Crocodile grinned, showing hundreds of sharp white teeth. "For my lunch today," he said, "I would like to eat a nice juicy little child."

The words that characters say sit inside the speech marks. Write out the speech from the bubbles below using punctuation.

I have secret plans and clever tricks

I hope it's not something nasty

Nasty! Of course it's not nasty! It's delicious.

Imagine the Enormous Crocodile meets a child. Write the conversation they might have below. Don't forget to add inverted commas, and choose words that the Enormous Crocodile might use!

Writing challenge

Write a story using one of the lines of speech above as the opening line. Remember to use speech marks around the words your characters say.

ASTONISHING APOSTROPHES

Apostrophes have two main uses when you're writing: to mark where letters are missing in contractions and to show possession.

Apostrophes are also used to make new words, showing where two words have been joined together into their contracted form. For example:

"is not" becomes "isn't"

"would have" becomes "would've"

Add the apostrophe in the correct place in these words

couldnt   **youre**   **lve**   **didnt**

Join together the two underlined words in each of the sentences below to make a new word.

Augustus, come away. You are dirtying my chocolate! _____

Be careful, Augustus! You are leaning out too far. _____

Save him! He will drown! _____

Do not just stand there! _____

Write what Augustus might be saying here. Can you use a contraction with an apostrophe?

_____

_____

_____

Apostrophes can be used to show possession – when something belongs to someone (or something).

If something belongs to one person or thing, an apostrophe with an "s" after it is placed at the end of the word:

Charlie's Golden Ticket

If something belongs to more than one person or thing and the word already ends in an "s", the apostrophe is placed right at the end of the word, after the "s":

The grandparents' beds

Tick the sentences with the correct apostrophes. Correct any sentences that are wrong.

- Verruca's gaze fell on a squirrel in the nut room.

- Next they visited Willy Wonkas' inventing room.

- They listened to the group of Oompa-Loompa's songs.

- The parents collected their childrens' coats.

You can use some possessive apostrophes to think of a new story! Choose one thing from each column to make an exciting, funny or silly story idea.

The girl's . . .	Golden Ticket . . .	was stolen.
The cat's . . .	greediness . . .	caused a lot of trouble.
Willy Wonka's . . .	happiness . . .	led to a terrible end.
Grandpa Joe's . . .	Whipple-Scrumptious Fudgemallow Delight . . .	fell in the sea.

PUTTING IT INTO PRACTICE

Hooray, you're nearly there! Now it's time to use all your new word wizardry to write a story of your own. This section has some writing activities to practise weaving wonderous words into superb stories.

Look back over the pages you've completed so far. Write down your favourite new words and any story ideas they lead to below.

Page 17 – Prefixes and suffixes

Page 25 – Creating characters

Page 29 – Amazing animals

Page 37 – Story structure

Page 39 – Story openings

Which box gives you the best idea for a story?

What title would you give your story?

FINISH THE SCENE

Read these scenes from some of Roald Dahl's stories, and then use your imagination to write what could happen next. Remember to use some of the words you've learned from this book.

James and the Giant Peach

And then suddenly, while he was doing this, he happened to notice that right beside him and below him, close to the ground, there was a hole in the side of the peach.

It was quite a large hole, the sort of thing an animal about the size of a fox might have made. James knelt down in front of it, and poked his head and shoulders inside.

He crawled in.

What happened next?

_____

_____

_____

_____

_____

_____

_____

_____

The Witches

I looked round and I saw a hideous painted and powdered witch's face staring down at me, and the face opened its mouth and yelled triumphantly, "It's here! It's behind the screen! Come and get it!" The witch reached out a gloved hand and grabbed me by the hair but I twisted free and jumped away.

What happened next?

Writing challenge

Use one of the scenes you've written in a brand new story.

A NEW ADVENTURE

It's time to flex your vocabulary by writing a new story featuring some well-loved Roald Dahl characters.

In *The Twits*, the Roly-Poly bird says he likes to travel as he can fly anywhere in the world. Where might the Roly-Poly bird go next, and what sort of adventures might he have?

Story plan

Characters:

Exciting thing that happens:

How the story ends:

Words to use:

Imagine that one day the small foxes from *Fantastic Mr Fox* decide to venture out of their hole to have an adventure. Write a new story with them in.

Story plan

Characters:

Exciting thing that happens:

How the story ends:

Words to use:

Writing challenge

Choose your favourite character from a Roald Dahl book, and create a new story for them. Perhaps you'll write about:

- What happens when Charlie and Willy Wonka try inventing a new sweet together?

- Another adventure for Danny set in Hazell's Wood?

- What happens when George makes another medicine?

BUILD A STORY!

Choose a word from each cloud (there's plenty of space for you to add lots of words of your own, too!). Then build an exciting story plan by following the path from one cloud to the next.

Once upon a time, there was a . . .

child
robot
kitten
superhero
monster

. . . who was very . . .

lonely.
kind.
powerful.
jealous.
shy.

At the end of the story, they . . .

. . . lived happily ever after.
. . . had won the battle!
. . . had made a new friend.
. . . were pleased everything had worked out.

. . . where they battled against . . .

an enemy.
their worries.
a big problem.
magic that went wrong.

Most of all, they wanted to . . .

visit
steal
conjure
own
help
find
overcome

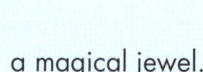

a magical jewel.
a new friend.
a safe home.
a terrible enemy.
a magical spell.

So, they travelled to a . . .

strange
busy
enchanted
terrifying
wonderful
deserted

planet
city
forest
cave
space station
land

WHOPPSY WORDS FOR...

In the next few pages, you'll find lots of words and phrases from Roald Dahl's incredible stories. Some are words that sound especially brilliant, and some are invented words! You can borrow them and use them in your own writing.

Before you start searching for inspiration, use this page to write down some ideas of your own.

My favourite hero from a book, TV programme, film or game is:

Words to describe how they **look**

Words to describe how they **move**

Words to describe their **emotions** and **feelings**

My favourite villain from a book, programme, film or game is:

Words to describe how they **look**

Words to describe how they **move**

Words to describe their **emotions** and **feelings**

HEROES

Find the perfect words to describe the heroes in your story.

There are lots of different ways to be a hero. Perhaps your hero will have special powers, like Matilda. Underline the words and phrases which help you to imagine Matilda's powers.

And now, quite slowly, there began to creep over Matilda a most extraordinary and peculiar feeling. The feeling was mostly in the eyes. A kind of electricity seemed to be gathering inside them. A sense of power was brewing in those eyes of hers, a feeling of great strength was settling itself deep inside her eyes. But there was also another feeling which was something else altogether, and which she could not understand. It was like flashes of lightning. Little waves of lightning seemed to be flashing out of her eyes. Her eyeballs were beginning to get hot, as though vast energy was building up somewhere inside them. It was an amazing sensation.

Or perhaps your hero is brave and determined like Sophie from *The BFG*.

Sophie had never felt so helpless in her life. After a while, she stood up and cried out, "I can't stand it! Just think of those poor children who are going to be eaten alive in a few hours' time! We can't just sit here and do nothing! We've got to go after those brutes!"

Here are some useful words and phrases for writing about a hero:

quick	gentle	brave	sparkled
lithe and agile	clever	gallant	twinkling eyes
tiny	impish	beamed	strong and muscular
determined	huge	danced	comforting

Create a hero for your story. Draw them below, write their name, and note down some useful words and phrases to describe them. Use the opposite page to help you!

MY HERO

USEFUL WORDS AND PHRASES

Hello, my name is

Write a description of your hero using your notes, your favourite words and phrases from this page, and your own ideas.

VILLAINS

Every story needs a good villain. Use the words and phrases on this page to create your own.

Perhaps your villain will have a monstrous appearance, like the giants from *The BFG*? Underline the words that help to make the Bloodbottler sound beastly.

The Bloodbottler was a gruesome sight. There was black hair sprouting on his chest and arms and on his stomach. The hair on his head was long and dark and tangled. His foul face was round and squashy-looking. The eyes were tiny holes. The nose was small. But the mouth was huge.

Or perhaps your villain will look ordinary, but have an evil nature, like witches? Underline your favourite words and phrases from *The Witches* that show how villainous they are.

REAL WITCHES dress in ordinary clothes and look very much like ordinary women. They live in ordinary houses and they work in ORDINARY JOBS.

That is why they are so hard to catch.

A REAL WITCH hates children with a red-hot sizzling hatred that is more sizzling and red-hot than any hatred you could possibly imagine [. . .] Her mind will always be plotting and scheming and churning and burning and whizzing and phizzing with murderous bloodthirsty thoughts.

Here are some useful words and phrases for writing about a villain:

deathly	**snarled**	**unblinking**	**burning with rage**
grotesque	**wolfish**	**talons**	**sour**
cold	**cruel**	**claw-like**	**fierce**

Create a villain for your story. Draw them below, write their name, and note down some useful words and phrases to describe them. Use the opposite page to help you!

MY VILLAIN

Hello, my name is

USEFUL WORDS AND PHRASES

Write a description of your villain below. Remember to choose your words carefully to tell your reader as much about their character and appearance as you can.

TIME

Choosing the correct words to describe the time of day or year in your story can create a wonderful sense of atmosphere and help your reader picture the scene.

Read the story text below from *The BFG*.

The witching hour, somebody had once whispered to her, was a special moment in the middle of the night when every child and every grown-up was in a deep deep sleep, and all the dark things came out from hiding and had the world to themselves.

WORDS FOR DIFFERENT TIMES OF DAY

morning	dawn	midnight
evening	sunset	midday
night	twilight	sunrise
dusk	the witching hour	afternoon

Write some ideas for what might happen in a story at different times of the day.

In the afternoon

At sunset

At

Choose one part of the day, and write the opening lines of a story set at that time. You could use the useful words and phrases in the boxes below, or choose words of your own.

MORNING

dawn	birdsong
first light	dawn chorus
sun's first rays	horizon
rising sun	rose
bathed in orange light	crept
	stretched
dew	spread
frost	waking

DAYTIME

sun

sunlight

cloudless sky

sun's path across the sky

highest point

bright

busy

working

NIGHT

moon	gloomy
stars	nocturnal
velvety-blackness	star-lit
inky	sunk
grey	fell beneath the horizon
moonlit	

Writing challenge

Write a story set in the witching hour. What sort of *dark things* might come out in your story?

THE SEASONS

Stories can happen at any time of year! Choosing the perfect words can help your reader to imagine the scene. It can also give you ideas for stories – your characters could have adventures in the snow or at the beach!

Read the story text below from *Danny the Champion of the World*. Underline the words and phrases that help to create an image of the scene.

> *"Your mother was a great one for walking, Danny. And she would always bring something home with her to brighten up the wagon. In the summer it was wildflowers or grasses. When the grass was in seed she could make it look absolutely beautiful in a jug of water, especially with some stalks of wheat or barley in between. In the autumn she would pick branches of leaves, and in the winter it was berries or old man's beard."*

> *It was a calm sunny evening with little wisps of brilliant white cloud hanging motionless in the sky, and the valley was cool and very quiet as the two of us began walking together along the road that ran between the hills towards Wendover.*

What season might it be in this part of the story? Write down the words and phrases that show you.

_____

_____

_____

_____

_____

There are lots of words to describe the different seasons. Read the words below, then write the opening sentence to a scene using words and phrases that will tell your reader what season it is.

SPRING
fresh, bright, green, verdant, lush, buds, bloom, daffodils, tulips, snowdrops, lambs gambolling

SUMMER
cloudless, brilliant, baking, balmy, scorching, fierce, butterflies dancing, crickets chirping, plants wilting

AUTUMN
golden, breezy, chill in the air, misty, foggy, cosy, crackling, harvest, rustling

WINTER
crisp, frosty, snowy, blizzard, slippery, chill, bitter, biting, freezing, hibernating

_____

_____

_____

_____

Writing challenge

Choose your favourite season, and write a story set then. Can you use plenty of descriptions of the weather and setting in your story?

EMOTIONS AND FEELINGS

Thinking carefully about the words you use to describe how your characters feel and act is very important when you're writing.

Write how the characters might feel in the below lines from *The Magic Finger*. You can use words and phrases in the box at the bottom of the page.

Philip and William began dancing about with joy.

_____

Mrs Gregg began to cry. "Oh, dear! Oh, dear!" she sobbed.

_____

I saw red. And before I was able to stop myself, I did something I never meant to do. I PUT THE MAGIC FINGER ON THEM ALL!

_____

	MORE WORDS FOR HOW THEY MIGHT FEEL	THINGS THEY MIGHT DO
HAPPY	joyful, jolly, content, delighted, thrilled, hopscotchy, gleeful	smile, laugh, grin, chuckle, giggle, skip, beam, snort, jump for joy
ANGRY	livid, cross, furious, annoyed, contemptuous, irritated, red mist	snarl, turn red in the face, glare, clench their fists, roar, rant
SCARED	frightened, fearful, alarmed, terrified, anxious, nervous	shake, tremble, quiver, break out in a cold sweat, freeze, shudder
SAD	upset, unhappy, heartbroken, depressed, miserable, forlorn	cry, sob, weep, tremble, tears run down their cheeks

Now write a sentence to show how each of these characters might feel and what they might do. Use words and phrases from the opposite page or think of some of your own.

A small boy on his first day at school:

_____

_____

_____

A penguin chick who has got lost on the ice:

_____

_____

_____

A strict headteacher who has just dropped her piece of toast in the mud:

_____

_____

_____

Writing challenge

Write a short story about a character who feels a very strong emotion. What sort of things might they do so the reader knows how they feel?

WONDERFUL WORD BANK

Congratulations! You've got to the end of this book and learned so many words! Use this space to write down any interesting new words you come across that you could use in your writing.